CONTENTS

P9-CRT-543

Some words are shown in bold, **like this.** You can find out what they mean by looking in the glossary.

COULD A ROBOT MAKE MY DINNER?

Robots are already used to make food in factories. So, if you have eaten a frozen dinner, then some sort of robot probably *did* make your dinner!

Scientists have also built robot chefs like the one in the photo, but these are rare and expensive. Who knows, one day, maybe everyone will have one!

This robot chef makes sushi with a hand that looks human!

COULD A ROBOT MAKE MY DINNER?

And Other Questions About Technology

Kay Barnham

Raintree

Chicago, Illinois

Edited by Dan Nunn, Rebecca Rissman,
   and John-Paul Wilkins
Designed by Steve Mead
Picture research by Mica Brancic
Production by Sophia Argyris
Originated by Capstone Global Library Ltd
Printed and bound in China by CTPS

17 16 15 14 13
10 9 8 7 6 5 4 3 2 1

Library of Congress Cataloging-in-Publication Data
Cataloging-in-Publication data is available at the
Library of Congress: loc.gov

ISBN 978-1-4109-5200-4 (hardback)
ISBN 978-1-4109-5206-6 (paperback)

Acknowledgments
We would like to thank the following for permission to
reproduce photographs: © Frank Pattyn, Laboratoire
de Glaciologie, Université Libre de Bruxelles p. 27;
Alamy pp. 15 (© Dmitry Mikhaevich), 20 (© PBWPIX), 21
(© Image Source), 29 (© Simon Belcher); Corbis p. 11
(Godong/© Philippe Lissac), 23 (© Roger Ressmeyer),
28 (epa/© Adrian Bradshaw); Getty Images pp. 17
(Gary Williams), 19 (Photolibrary/Rune Johansen);
NASA p. 7; Rex Features p. 4 (Sinopix); Shutterstock pp.
5 (© Leonid Shcheglov), 6 (© Hunor Focze), 8 laptop
(© iQoncept), 8 bedding (© karam Miri), 9 (© Dmitriy
Shironosov), 10 living room (© art&design), 10 magician
(© Elnur), 12 painter (© auremar), 12 toothbrush (©
Ioannis Pantzi), 13 (© Leah-Anne Thompson), 14
cartoon weight (© Robert Spriggs), 14 crane (© Tonis
Pan), 16 computer (© Fer Gregory), 16 goggles (©
Rtimages), 16 aeroplane (© PJF), 18 tyrannosaurus (©
DM7), 18 person in chemical protection suit (© 3355m),
18 spacecraft (© Jan Kaliciak), 22 futuristic space
station (© Andreas Meyer), 22 astronaut (© siraphat),
22 nappy (© Ogonkova), 24 pirate (© Jeanne
McRight), 24 house in water (© Lightspring), 25 (©
nevenm), 26 snow-capped peaks (© Vadim Petrakov),
26 man holding measuring tape (© luiggi33).

Cover photographs of robot chef (© Julien Tromeur),
cheeseburger (© Valentyn Volkov), and French
fries (© Aaron Amat) reproduced with permission
of Shutterstock.

We would like to thank Diana Bentley and Marla Conn
for their invaluable help in the preparation of this book.

Every effort has been made to contact copyright
holders of any material reproduced in this book. Any
omissions will be rectified in subsequent printings if
notice is given to the publisher.

These robots are making delicious ice cream cones!

WHY DO WE NEED ROCKETS TO GET INTO SPACE?

We need rockets to escape the pull of Earth's **gravity**. When a rocket is launched, powerful engines burn rocket fuel. Nozzles point **gases** and flames from the engines downward. This gives enough **thrust** to speed the rocket upward and into space.

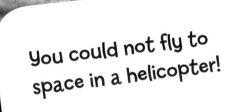

You could not fly to space in a helicopter!

7

CAN A COMPUTER REALLY CATCH A VIRUS?

Absolutely! But a computer virus is not a disease. It is actually a computer program that spreads from one computer to another, often by e-mail. Just as human viruses can make us sick, computer viruses can harm computers. Some viruses stop computers from working properly. Others delete information stored on them.

Did you know? A computer virus leaves a copy of itself on each computer it affects.

DO REMOTE CONTROLS WORK BY MAGIC?

Sadly, they do not! Remote controls work by sending out beams of **infrared** light. They can be used to operate TVs, sound systems, and other devices. Different buttons send different signals—for example, to change the channel or turn up the volume. But we cannot see infrared light, so the beams are invisible to us!

Did you know?
Some video game consoles use infrared light in their wireless controllers.

HOW DO THE STRIPES GET INTO TOOTHPASTE?

To make striped toothpaste, tubes are filled with big stripes of different colored toothpaste. Then, the end of the tube is sealed, to keep it inside. When the tube is squeezed, small amounts of each color are pushed out of the nozzle. These appear as long, much thinner stripes.

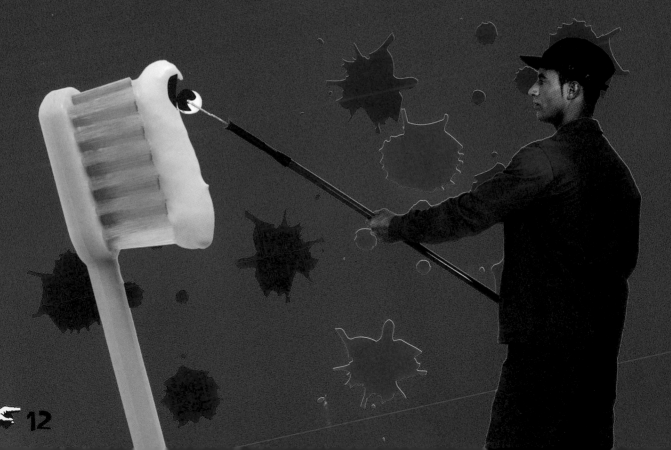

Toothpaste is very slippery. When the tube is squeezed, the colors slide past each other and do not get mixed up.

WHY DON'T CRANES FALL OVER?

It is all about balance. To stop it from falling over, a crane needs to create enough force to balance the load it is picking up.

Tower cranes have a short arm that carries a weight and a long arm with a hook for picking things up. As long as the weight and the load are balanced, the crane will not fall over.

VERY HEAVY

weight

load

WHO FLIES A PILOTLESS AIRPLANE?

Unmanned aerial vehicles—also called UAVs or drones—have computers on board, so they can fly themselves. They can also be flown by human pilots. But these pilots are down on the ground, not up in the air. UAVs are sent to places where it would be too risky for humans to go.

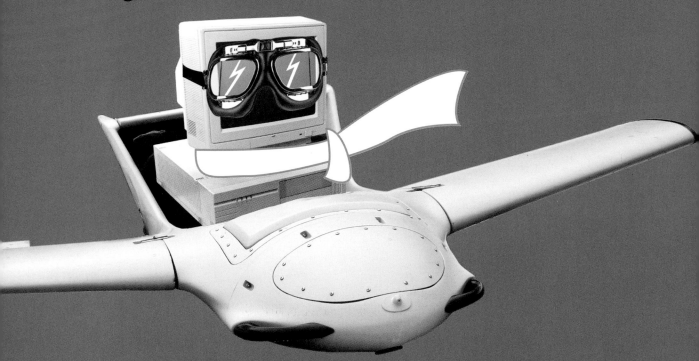

It looks as if these pilots are playing computer games, but they are actually flying real aircraft.

IS TIME TRAVEL POSSIBLE?

Yes. But don't get *too* excited. The closer you get to the speed of light, the slower time gets. So, if you were able to travel at millions of miles per hour, your watch would go a tiny bit slower and you would travel a little bit into the future. But going back in time is impossible.

It is easier to watch time travel in a sci-fi movie than it is to do it in real life.

Did you know?
Scientists at the CERN laboratory have managed to make **particles** travel at speeds close to the speed of light. It would be much more difficult to make people travel that quickly!

WHY DO I NEED SPECIAL GLASSES TO WATCH 3D MOVIES?

A **3D** movie is not one movie, but rather two! Each one is slightly different. 3D glasses have two different **lenses**, so you see one movie through one lens and the other movie through the other lens. Your brain puts the two images together to make a movie look like real 3D.

Did you know?
3D glasses make objects in 3D movies appear nearer or farther away, just like our eyes see objects (or 'judge distance') in real life!

HOW DO ASTRONAUTS USE A TOILET IN SPACE?

There is no **gravity** in space, which means that everything floats. So, if astronauts used a normal toilet, things could get very messy! Instead, astronauts use a special toilet or a pipe that uses air rather than water to flush waste away.

Did you know?
During liftoff, landing, and on spacewalks, it is difficult to get to a space toilet. So, astronauts wear adult diapers!

WHY DON'T BOATS SINK?

It is because of the weight of a boat and the amount of water it **displaces**.

A boat weighing 100 tons sinks into the water until it has displaced 100 tons of water. Then, if there is still some of the boat above the water, it floats!

Oh no!

Houses do not float well!

Some of a boat's **hull** is under the water, out of sight.

HOW DO I MEASURE A MOUNTAIN?

Can you imagine trying to measure a mountain with a ruler? It would not be easy! Instead, you can measure **angles** between the ground and the mountaintop. Then, you can use a special formula to figure out the height. Today, scientists also use measurements from **satellites**, which are even easier and more accurate!

theodolite

The angle between the ground and a mountaintop can be measured with a device called a theodolite.

WHY DO NIGHT-VISION GOGGLES MAKE EVERYTHING GREEN?

Night-vision goggles make even the smallest amount of light thousands of times brighter. First, the eyepiece makes the image bigger. Then, it is shone onto a screen coated with a glow-in-the-dark substance called phosphor. This is what makes everything look green!

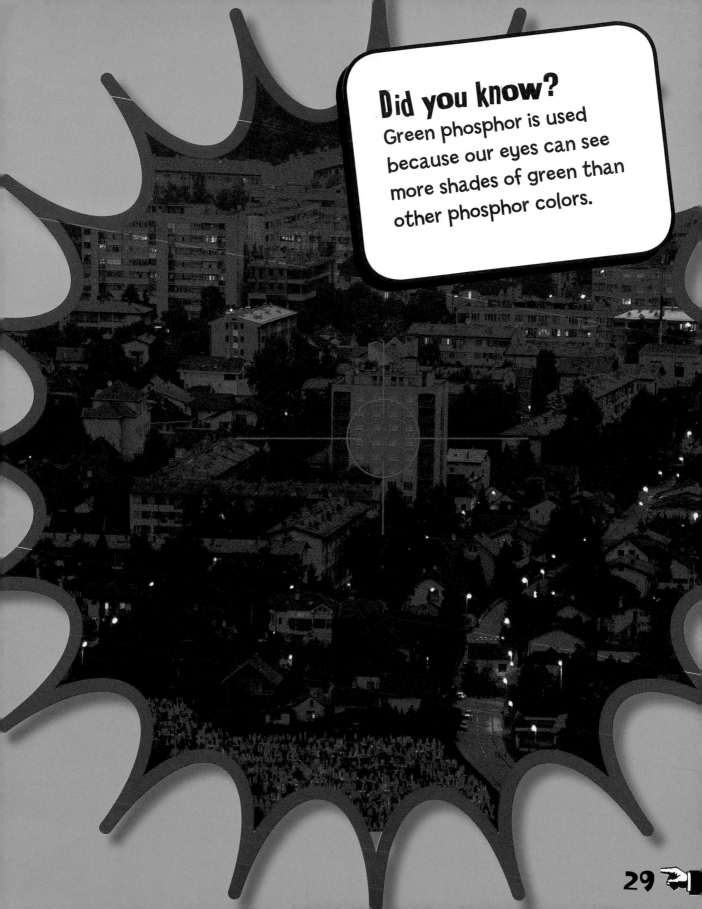

Did you know?
Green phosphor is used because our eyes can see more shades of green than other phosphor colors.

GLOSSARY

3D something that has three dimensions—height, width, and depth—like objects do in real life

angle size of the corner where two lines meet

displace push out of the way; move elsewhere

gas substance like air that can move around freely

gravity force that pulls everything toward Earth

hull outer shell of a boat

infrared type of light wave not visible to the human eye

lens curved piece of glass or plastic that light can pass through

liquid something runny, like water

particle very, very tiny thing

satellite object that travels around Earth and collects information

solid hard or firm

thrust push

FIND OUT MORE

Books

Bell-Rehwoldt, Sheri. *Science Experiments That Surprise and Delight: Fun Projects for Curious Kids.* Mankato, Minn.: Capstone, 2011.

Brent Sandvold, Lynette. *Time for Kids Super Science Book.* New York: Time for Kids, 2009.

Harrison, Paul. *Space (Up Close).* New York: Rosen, 2008.

Web sites

Facthound offers a safe, fun way to find Internet sites related to this book. All of the sites on Facthound have been researched by our staff.

Here's all you do:
Visit www.facthound.com
Type in this code: 9781410952004

INDEX